Past Lives

Incredible Past Life Experiences

Davina DeSilver

DEDICATION

I feel privileged to have shared special moments with
clients, friends & family & all those who have touched
their soul and danced with their spirit

CONTENTS

1 INTRODUCTION

I have been shocked, elated, stunned and at times frozen with fear.

These are my experiences, never anyone famous, just real experiences of past lives, usually, though not always, with some pertinent reminder or similarity with events in my current life.

Can I prove the existence of past lives, no am I going to try, no - this is just a simple sharing about the things I have, seen and felt. I am no actress and no prima donna, in fact I hate fuss and bother of any kind, had I known I was going to be reeling about convinced I was in pain or crying so much in front of a crowd of fellow students I probably would never have signed up for the course. But a part of me wanted to know. I wanted to know for real, not be told about it by someone else.

Believing in the philosophy of 'better out than in' and being a bit of a natural sceptic I also knew I would only truly believe if I experienced things for myself . If things came up that needed to be dealt with, I didn't want to pretend they weren't there or sweep them under the carpet, I was ready to let go.

2 PAST LIFE REGRESSION THERAPY

My experiences of the existence of past lives has never been for entertainment purposes. I have loved being able to touch my spirit and that of others. Within all of us, lies the potential to access ancient memories, and times long past. I do believe that the body holds onto such memories, even if we don't consciously know how.

There is an intelligence in every single cell of our bodies. The mind is not the brain, it includes the brain but it is not limited to it. The brain is the physical organ, the mind is less tangible. It expands further than we think and communicates in ways I believe we have yet to master or fully understand.

There may be things in this life that just don't make sense to you, a recurring thought or dream that seems to bear no relevance to your current life. Sometimes specific aches, pains and physical imbalances may not be confined to an event in this current lifetime. If that is the case for you, you will know it in your heart *and* in your gut as you read these words. Using the sensations and feeling ability of the body is one of the ways we can access these deeply held memories, thoughts and beliefs. It's as if they are frozen in time, crystallised if you like, especially if they are associated with strong emotions and events.

The emotions, thoughts and beliefs at the time of death are particularly important and telling. Just as the consciousness of a baby responds to life and sounds outside of the womb before birth so does our consciousness at the point of death... and beyond.

As the soul experiences lifetime after lifetime, these strong residual memories can also be recreated; a chronic throat condition may relate to a previous hanging or strangulation. A frozen shoulder might correspond with an old bullet wound for example or an irrational fear of water might suggest a previous experience of drowning. These things may not make much sense in your modern day context but the energy behind them can be holding you back from living a peaceful life.

Such memories can be brought into our conscious awareness by different emotional states; by depression or anxiety, stress and phobias, even recurring relationship difficulties, nightmares and obsessions. I certainly found this to be true not only for myself but in others too. It's as if an energetic ripple from the past slowly edges in, to make itself known in some way in our current life. When we recognise it for what it is and are drawn to regression, we can follow the tell tale threads that reverberate in this life and find ourselves in times long since past; tasting an experience we thought was long forgotten.

I know in my heart what I have experienced in my own past life experiences and that of my fellow students and clients is true. I have never entered a past life seeking proof; I suppose I have been much more selfish than that. I wanted to feel it for myself, I wanted understanding and I wanted to feel the truth of it. I didn't want to enter the process with preconceived ideas or specific expectations.

I was prepared to walk away knowing I had tried it, if it turned out to be false or a little too flaky for me. At the time of my life I took my training, I believe the work I did with my spirit and soul ultimately helped me to become much more rounded and not only more nurturing and protective of my own energy but that of others too.

It is a beautiful privilege to work with the spirit, in whatever guise, as healer, therapist or even reading auras. You'll see in the book *The Human Aura - Reading Auras & Colors* that although people were originally drawn to having their aura read for fun, usually when we had finished the reading they had discovered a whole lot more about themselves than just if they were 'a red' or 'a blue'.

3 IT'S NOT FOR EVERYONE

Regression is not for everyone and it is not a magical elixir to solve every problem we have. But it can be very profound and will certainly suit some more than others. If it appeals to you, I am sure the opportunity will arise for you to experience it. When there is a pulling in your heart and the thought just won't seem to go away that is usually a good indicator it will be of use to you.

For me, regression therapy started a wonderful journey of working with spirit. I qualified with my diploma in regression therapy first and only then did I start my hypnosis training. I studied energy and became a Reiki Master and that lead on to all sorts of other energy related workshops and seminars, from reading auras to dealing with negative entities. Even to working with the tarot, not so much as a means of divination but I love how the images reveal profound insights about our consciousness and the story of life and how we evolve and grow over time.

In this book, I share a few of my experiences and on occasion use quotes taken directly from class notes recorded by my fellow pupils at the time. It's a combination of sharing the past life, whilst explaining a little about the technique and psychology behind it so you can see how the experience can be of benefit to those that find the idea appealing.

Contra Indicators

There are some instances where regression is not recommended and should even be avoided; the most common are listed below. It is always worth checking these out before considering past life regression.

People unable to think rationally and clearly, severely depressed, those with anorexic or schizophrenic symptoms, people taking high dosages of anti depressants or anti anxiety drugs.

Heart problems or fits and seizures can also be prohibitive as some memories can hold a lot of charge, invoking powerful emotions and sensations.

4 WHAT IS PAST LIFE REGRESSION THERAPY?

How do we remember and where do we store those memories? These are such big questions that could keep the greatest minds debating for lifetimes. There is no definitive short answer, things that we think are long forgotten can be recalled by any of our senses; sound, smell, taste, touch or sight.

They can be stored in the depths of our minds for years, seemingly dormant until a catalyst reawakens them. Many of our experiences and memories hold no specific charge for us and can be pleasant, warm recollections, some however can not only hold an emotional charge but they can also be destructive or limiting in some way.

Often it is not the memories themselves but the associations and connections we add to them that make them restrictive or limiting. To an outsider these can seem irrational, even ridiculous yet they are all so real to the person involved.

It is when such thoughts are unhelpful to our current lives that regression can be helpful.

Past life regression is a technique used to gain access to these deepest memories and resonances, whether real or imagined.

Once they are accessed and the underlying story revealed, a new level of understanding can be attained. Not only understanding, for when we use regression as a therapy we go beyond merely watching the scene. We work with it, employing specific techniques to allow the client to 'put right' or make adjustments to these memories so that they can bring peace and healing to the situation.

In this way, directly communicating with the subconscious mind, there is usually a positive effect noticed in the person's current life. It's as if they have been able to shift a burden in their energy and move on feeling much freer and lighter.

What can it do for me?

Past life regression often works where conventional methods do not or where the symptoms noted do not make much sense. These can be anything from recurring thoughts, problems, dreams or fears. The sort of thing that you know rationally doesn't seem to stack up and yet somehow they just won't go away.

Many therapies use the creative ability of the mind, to provide answers and the stimulus for change. It is here our flashes of insight and inspiration arrive and left unchecked, it is also here that our thoughts can run riot and we can find ourselves worrying about things that in actuality will never happen, yet we allow these fears to block our lives and prevent us from doing so much in life.

NLP uses the positive use of imagery to effect changes in a variety of creative ways; from reducing negative images in our mind to adding colour and feeling to the positive images we *do* want. The power of metaphors and the imagery associated with them is also well documented and practiced.

When we communicate with the subconscious mind it does not require facts and figures to make sense of things, its language is much more sensory and visual. Repeated messages are soon embedded and can become beliefs over time. Beliefs are powerful thoughts which underpin much of our lives, some we are consciously aware of and many we are not. The most powerful of these can be the beliefs about ourselves and our ability, our appearance and performance.

The mind holds the key to the store house of these thoughts, memories and beliefs, with new perspectives and understanding we can change many things, we can evaluate and discern. We can make decisions and choices to stay the same or change. In order to do this though, we need to be consciously aware of such thoughts and past life regression can surface them *and* the associated beliefs, shedding light on long forgotten threads that may well be affecting you today.

Those threads can be untied and rewoven bringing a sense of resolution, completion and peace, not just to a specific situation but to the attitude the subconscious has around it too. This is where you can notice beneficial changes to your everyday life you are experiencing right now.

In a therapeutic setting we accumulate facts and facets of the story which directly relate to the specific symptoms of the client. These are for personal discovery and empowerment and it is important to understand the story of the past life, to be able to navigate it to the point of death in that lifetime and then beyond. For it is in the afterlife that we can spend a great deal of time in the regression session as it is here that we can invite healing and compassionate understanding. This is the aspect I feel, that brings immense peace to clients and it is a wonderful privilege to share that space with them.

As therapists we are not interested in proving what is uncovered by the client, we respect the validity of their experiences, whether real or imagined. Regression sessions can be very powerful, emotive, humbling *and* empowering. It requires a deep level of trust and sharing. To be invited into the inner world that holds so much meaning and importance for the individual is an honour. We work with the imagery of the client's mind however it wishes to present itself, always keeping the goal of the therapy in mind.

There are however many studies that have followed regressions and **have** been conducted with a more fact finding and scientific approach. These studies have traced the facts given by the people regressed to check the validity of statements or claims made where possible. One of the most notable studies being *Twenty Cases Suggestive of Reincarnation* by Dr Ian Stevenson and the story of Arthur Flowerdew whose past life memories helped archaeologists with missing parts of their knowledge of Petra, a city in Jordan.

What can it be used for?

Although we don't need a reason or a symptom to experience a past life, some of the things that have responded well to using regression as a therapy are:

- Depression
- Irrational fears/thoughts
- Phobias & panic attacks
- Re occurring Relationship Problems
- Experiencing feelings of detachment and separateness
- Flash backs from dreams/ recurring images

"In summary Regression Therapy works with the psychological, somatic and spiritual unresolved residues from our present life and past lives. It is a comprehensive method for transforming them in a way that is both safe and structured." Andy Tomlinson *An Insight into Past Life Regression*

5 THE ENERGY BODY

Living in the modern Western World, it can be hard for us to appreciate the realm of regression because we are dealing with a world of thought, images, sensations and feelings. We deal less with the physical body and more with the energy of the subtle body.

The subtle body can be complex to explain and I'll try to keep things brief and give you my experience and impressions of it. It is an interesting topic to explore, should you feel so inclined. You'll find some suggested titles for further reading listed in the resource page. Much of what we know today has originated from books on ancient wisdom.

The Subtle Energy Body

The energy body is often described as being outside of the body but it cannot purely exist outside of us as our bodies are creating pulsations, energy and movement every second of every day. We have cells renewing, blood pumping, organs working and chemical reactions taking place constantly. All this energy not only fills our internal bodies but it extends beyond the physical frame too.

Within this energetic field, we find the resonance of our thoughts and emotions and everything that makes up our lives and life experiences. All of these things create our energetic signature or essence and each one of us is totally unique.

It's as if time is not a concept in this energy field, what happened yesterday, last year or fifty years ago, does not just drop off and wither away, it's still there. The language of energy is there for us all to interpret and it can be worked with, appreciated and understood.

Being ethereal in nature it can be difficult for our rational brain to comprehend at times but if you think how irrational you can be when you're madly in love or incredibly angry you'll understand how the intangible can be incredibly powerful.

There is a lot we can do to work with our energy system and many healing practices exist which include this important aspect of ourselves; from Reiki, to Acupuncture, and most alternative healing practices.

It's not about ignoring the physical body, it's about understanding that we are more than just skin and bones and to not address the energetic body is simply leaving the greater part of ourselves unaccounted for.

Just as when in life we deal with our emotions, it's not the emotion itself so much as the energy behind it; the fuel and intensity we feel will determine our actions and the resulting consequences.

Energy Centres

There are various centres or hubs within the energy body as well as layers. The hubs are better known as the chakras, there being seven main chakra centres to the human body. The various layers connect to the different aspects of our psyche; mentally, emotionally, physically and spiritually. So you can appreciate that the energy body is a holistic way of encompassing the many aspects of what it means to be human.

It is located within this field that the memories lie which we uncover and explore in past life regression, often releasing long held emotions and energy. So as well as regression techniques we will often use energy techniques, similar to those used in healing as it is all ultimately energy that we are dealing with.

Things are energy before they appear in the physical world, hence if we can relieve energetic blockages and restrictions, then things can run more smoothly not just in the clients energy but usually in their day to day life too.

It is in the energy field that old memories can be stored about past wounds for example and clients may report physical ailments or scars which correspond to previous methods of death. This can be as simple as a scar or birthmark or sometimes a sensation of having to swallow a lot or a feeling of restriction around the throat which when regressed reveals a previous experience of drowning or being hung.

Again research by Dr Ian Stevenson seemed to suggest that this was the case in his book *Where Reincarnation and Biology Intersect,* following the many studies he made.

6 LOVE, POISON & DEATH

This is my personal account of some of my own experiences of past lives and past life regression.

I can accept the existence of past lives and have felt and seen such things and yet I don't allow it to rule my current life and nor do I make excuses for this current existence because of any previous life events and circumstances.

My real journey started with my own personal regression. I'm not sure what I expected as I had nothing much to judge it by but here's an account of that session.

Having filled in the obligatory forms and briefly discussed what might unfold and the sort of current situations I was experiencing, the session began with a simple relaxation process. It's important to let you know, I'm actually quite a shy person and not one for great shows of emotion or outburst. I like my own company and am not the greatest 'group' person or confider of personal stuff so this was quite a big deal for me.

The only thing I did know was, I wanted to **really know** - I wanted to be open to whatever was going to unfold, I was determined that I would not get in my own way and if it meant having to talk or share then I would do it. I just needed to know.

What I don't think I was mentally prepared for though was the actual bodily feelings and sensations I got - and I mean real bodily sensations! There was I , quiet, shy and thirty something, going through the regression process and then wham! In seconds I was writhing about on the couch as if I was in pain. The pain felt real although I knew it wasn't happening to me right then, but my body was having spasms as if I was retching and I was gripping on to my stomach. Talk about being convinced.

My eyes were still closed and yet the images I could 'see' were so real - the best way I can describe it is it's just like recalling a memory - a vivid memory and somehow the body remembers at the same time - with its own physical reaction. So you're not watching a scene - you're in it too, yet with the help of the person guiding you, you can navigate and dip into and out of it very safely.

My guide was my future tutor and I knew I was in safe hands, I trusted him and his approach. When asked what was happening I told him - I described what I was feeling, where I was and the set of circumstances that led me to this place;

Initially I viewed the scene from above. I could see the room; there was a bare wooden floor, wooden walls, and people were gathered around the bed. The window was open, I wasn't aware of there being any glass. There was the noise of a busy village going on outside and the view stretched out over expansive fields with a woodland to the right, on the brow of a hill.

After a few minutes and some gentle questioning from my guide, I realised it was me. I was the one lying on the bed.

I was surrounded by my family, writhing in the deadly grip of a poison I had just taken. I had done this to myself and my last thoughts revolved around feelings of defiance and indignation. "I'd rather end my life than live by wrong principles and ridiculous compromise".

I was in France, in a village, my father was a man of authority and standing, similar to being a mayor is how I described it. I, being his daughter was expected to act in certain ways, which generally speaking I was happy to do. I loved village life and followed my father who led by example and I did the same. The trouble was an arranged marriage that I was supposed to be going ahead with. I just couldn't and wouldn't do it. And I could not believe that my father was the one demanding that it happen, not shifting at all from what he saw as his duty and mine.

What my father didn't know was, my heart and soul were with my love, an artist, a beautiful soul who lived in the woods on the outskirts of the village. He would never have been considered a suitable match.

I could see his face and at the same time could sense his personality and how it felt to be around him. We were enveloped in such love that anything seemed possible. How on earth could I ever be expected to give that up and accept this older suitor who made 'sense' to the family and the prospect of succession? A good, sensible but loveless alliance would never suit me - the day I accepted that I knew would be the day I died inside.

The passion and helplessness I felt were enormous, there was an overwhelming sense of it being unjust but at least I was in charge of this; my death. I had decided that it would not happen their way. I saw no joy in the life that was being chosen for me, so better to end it now than live a diminished life.

This hadn't been a long and thought out decision; this was all decided in the aftermath of a tremendous argument with my father.

I was aware of watching this scene, almost as if viewing it from above, looking down and somehow being aware of all of the threads of the story that led me to that place of deciding suicide was the only option. I could also feel the emotions tangled up in the story and knew that the girl in the story, although she looked different to me now, she was undoubtedly me, the essence of me.

From this position I was also able to see the fact that I was unknowingly with child at the time, and able to feel and see the distress it caused my family and my father in particular. He had such love for me in that lifetime and yet his pride and position prevented him from being able to express that love in a way, I his daughter could tangibly feel. The strange thing was I had known he loved me, the overriding sense was how ridiculous and wrong it was to live a compromised life, whilst expounding the propriety of life and setting good principles to live by. With his stature and standing it was as if those good principles had become the very thing to be his own undoing as well as my own and my unborn child, let alone the rest of the family.

It was as if we had become slaves to our duty and position; at the cost of our own feelings and emotions.

As my guide asked me more questions about how I was feeling, what I was wearing, what I could hear and see, the sensations and experience became more and more real for me.

It's hard to describe the gamut of emotions I felt; I wept, I cried out, I was doubled up in pain, I felt a sense of loss, I tasted fear and swallowed anger. It's a bit like the whole of the life flashes before your eyes and as the images arrive they are accompanied by the associated feelings. You can feel them when prompted, dropping in to the character and you can also pull back to see the bigger picture, gaining a new level of insight and understanding. By the end of it I was exhausted and yet relieved, something very good had happened and I felt a great sense of inner peace and contentment.

During the session at times I felt totally embodied into that character of the time and at others, when guided I could dissociate from her and view the situation more dispassionately, as if from my own higher self. This is a characteristic of the way we were taught to guide the past life therapy sessions, as it is a therapeutic process, not merely idle entertainment.

The idea being that any unresolved business is tactfully dealt with; it is surfaced and discussed, with whatever feels right to be done, being done, to ensure that the energy of that spirit, me as the young woman in that life could now rest easy. Any stuck or residual energy held in those past life memories could be affecting my current life in some way, as the concept of time is pretty much irrelevant when we engage with the soul.

What was interesting was some of the other characters involved in that story. I recognised different aspects of them in some of the people in my current life. The father in that life time, in his strict aspect, one of position, duty and obligation, he had the energy of my husband in this current life - when he was being overbearing and dominant. The young man, living in the woods was also my husband but his energy when he was younger, the energy of the man I fell in love with, the artist, the innocent love we shared with the promise of a wonderful future.

It was interesting to see myself torn between these aspects; love and duty, freedom and obligation, creativity and rigidity. This certainly echoed my current life at the time. How often do we impose our own limitations, judgements and expectations, many times to an unattainable degree?

I was amazed at how strong the images were, the feelings and the physical sensations I had felt in my body. It is a lot to take in as it is quite a bizarre experience; you become the actor and the audience in your own play. In a second you get images and insights that have so much information attached to them it is hard to put into words. Having to describe what you see and feel to the guide sometimes feels like it slows the process down, yet at the same time it enables you to see things more fully. You don't get lost in the process this way and you don't feel overwhelmed. It does take time to integrate what you learn and experience, especially if up until that point you were as new to the idea as I was about the possible existence of past lives.

I'd been able to describe my clothes, the room I was in, the people around me, who was there as that body in that lifetime drew her last breath and the effect that had on the family. We also spent some time calling in the energy of the unborn child and the other characters of the story, to be able to clear the decks so to speak. To discover why the father was so harsh, to apologise to the baby, to express love to my family and to speak with my father, forgive him and him forgive me. Reparation and forgiveness brought a sense of peace and calmness; I was able to rest easy, as was everyone else involved.

After such an involved session you can feel quite wiped out afterwards, not to mention needing time to sort out in your mind what you see and feel and how it reflects on current events. Did it fix my marriage - no - in fact I think it was part of my journey in leaving that partnership; realising abuse and bullying were no substitutes for love. That's not to say as a direct result of past life regression I divorced my husband but over the next few years I changed, I became more me. I also became much stronger.

I realised what I would and would not accept and I undertook quite lengthy training as a therapist, although I had not previously intended this. First and foremost I was there for my own healing. I was in a place where I wanted and could handle quite intense healing and was prepared to do whatever it took to help that process.

By learning to become a therapist I was learning the process, feeding my mind, understanding the reasoning why it worked or why a certain process was recommended whilst receiving the therapies and experiencing what it's like to be the client. Becoming a therapist was a massive second to me, personal healing and change was my main driver. Funnily though I think this helped me with clients, it's not about the therapy it's about the person, the individual, their spirit, their energy and their essence.

On most of my courses this was counter to the other trainees, they were already therapists of some kind but I knew I didn't want 2 or 3 sessions of healing - I wanted 3 years or more! For me it has been important to mentally understand the process and procedures and then I can relax into the therapy much more. I don't think we ever 'get the t shirt'; we are always work in progress, it's not about being 'fixed' it's about growth and becoming more of who we truly are.

Some of my other past life experiences were not so intense, some were more so. Sometimes, I'd get a sense of just moments in time and in others I would see more of the story. Many made me cry tears I thought would never stop, other didn't make much sense and on quite a few I didn't go quite where the therapist wanted me to go to and ended up having some weird and wonderful channelling experiences and even some non human ones which again took me by surprise.

7 MANY WAYS TO DIE

In several of my past lives, I would recognise other characters and I often shared experiences with people I knew from this life time. One time I sensed my two daughters, who were also my daughters in that previous life. I didn't get the entire life history but the scene that held the strongest charge was where they had waded out into a lake to pull my dead body back to shore.

Our home then was a simple wooden building, built close to the lakeside and a wooded area to the rear. I had been strangled and throttled as a woman in my thirties and my spirit felt the energy as the girls gently took me back to shore. I hadn't put up much of a fight and the body and strength of will was both tired and weak.

What was interesting was the sensation of floating at the same time as a heaviness of spirit, a profound sadness at the realisation that death was almost a welcome respite from that daily life.

I feel it is important to note here that I am not nor never have been suicidal! When encountering past lives and in the manner in which I was taught, we will always experience the death point and often that is the very point we enter the experience, as it carries so much significance and charge.

Our attitudes to death and dying are often not explored much and can be something we try and put off thinking about, almost believing that just by talking about it we are somehow tempting fate. Certainly it is not something that we generally talk openly about.

"It is, I believe, our drastically limited version of life that prevents us from accepting or even beginning seriously to think about the possibility of rebirth." Sogyal Rinpoche, *The Tibetan Book of Living and Dying*.

In this kind of regression therapy it is important to know the dying thoughts and beliefs. To check when that last breath is taken, so that any relevant vibration or frequency of thought and emotion can be better examined and understood, and more than likely, released. That death point is worked through depending on the individual client and then if it is appropriate more details are looked into regarding the story of the life leading up to that point. Once that is done we will go beyond the death point, to follow the path of the spirit or energy, to see what if anything needs doing, saying or releasing.

Although there is a lot of death going on - it is a truly beautiful experience or at least it can be. You absorb a profound feeling of love and trust and personally I love working with my own spirit in this way and the spirit of others too. When you can truly bare your soul and entrust the energy of your spirit to someone, you cannot help but be touched and embraced by a deep sense of sharing and compassionate love.

Some of the experiences we met on our training sessions were just snatches in time, depending on what the focus of the lesson was at the time, although usually we were encouraged to let the full story unfold and clear unfinished business as we went along.

Occasionally you see fragments from several lives, or dissociate from one to another, that can be for a whole host of reasons. This chapter is full of such snippets; some are taken directly from class notes made by other trainees observing the process.

There was one instance when I recalled being burnt at the stake, bit of a cliché I know but it's true.

The story started with me feeling a great pressure around my chest area.

"It's red...angry...my heart is beating much more strongly..this is unjust.."

As we examined that feeling and where the pressure was coming from I described being outside and having to push a massive wooden log, round and round - it was a similar set up to what you might imagine a horse or donkey being strapped to but the brute animal force was coming from humans. We had to walk round and round, pushing this wooden pole. It was obviously part of some early kind of primitive machinery; it felt like it was ultimately grinding something down. I was a slave in that lifetime and was angry at having been born into such a predicament.

"I have to keep it going or I get whipped. The guard wears skins, he is up higher than me" There was a simple wooden structure, with the guards being able to walk on a higher level, walking around the enclosure, watching to make sure the momentum was kept up.

In this instance I was being asked to describe how I was feeling and the emotion of the moment, which was a mixture of anger and indignation. As I was trying to describe these, I was aware of another experience, it continued on from the turning round and round of pushing that log, to a giddy sensation of spinning. Suddenly I was seeing a very different lifetime but the emotions and feelings were similar.

Although you can answer someone in the trance-like state you are in with regression, your words don't tend to flow as in normal speech. It is a strange but not unpleasant experience. For me, I would find I was aware of a great many things, sensations, images, and feelings, trying to find words to clearly express what you sense and feel can be hard. The interesting thing is your language tends to be very simple, almost childlike in some cases. Your guide in regression needs to constantly ask questions to get a sense of the story and what needs to be done but they can also ask things that at times are totally irrelevant and can sometimes pull you out of the experience.

A lot depends on your intention for the regression and the purpose of the session.

In this session I moved from the spinning round and round, pushing this huge wooden pole round and round and round, to a sense of spinning in my head, feeling a sense of disorientation, to the question "What's going on for you now?" I answered;

" Spinning...spinning...stood up......hands are tied behind me........(sharp intake of breath, as realisation struck)....going to be burned...........3 of us...... an example.....given up......everyone else has gone......I want to die....... throwing stones...... I hate these people (struck by a rock to the head)"

In situations like this, timing is very important, the person guiding you can interrupt your flow of images and information or they can tease more out of you. Even to recall it now as I type, I can recall the woozy feeling, the spinning sensation, almost I suppose on the edge of consciousness, head bowed forward, beaten, defeated, disheartened yet still a sense of valour within. In this instance, as with the pole pushing - I was a man in this lifetime.

"Getting hard to breathe now..... smells of burning flesh...feet are burning but I can't feel them...smoke everywhere... woman and child on stakes too... child needs help...so much is going on...."

Further questioning led me to explain how I had wanted to protect and help the others, but couldn't, the dying thoughts and feelings were ones of despair and anger - anger at a world where such things could happen. "I've let them down."

I only had one other experience of being burnt at the stake, again there were three of us sharing the same fate. I had hardly any story attached to this but the image was so clear and strong. I remember silently looking across at my fellow captives; we had been set up somehow. My hands tied behind me, the fires not yet lit and a crowd gathering to watch the event. There seemed such power and relevance in my looking to my right hand side across to my fellow victims, words were not necessary and could not have done the situation justice. Looking straight into the other's eyes we accepted our fate without accepting a thing.

We had been protectors of something or someone, not soldiers as such although we had fought for a cause.

My impression was that we had worked for people in power and now that power had been turned against us. I never explored that lifetime any more than that, these experiences were not for fact finding or attempting to prove or disprove anything, they were simply part of my ongoing training. What has always amazed me though is at how very real and emotionally charged they can be. You can walk into a room as a thirty something woman with a notepad and pen and leave having been, whipped, tortured, burnt at the stake as a man, woman or child - feeling that something wonderful has just gone on, even if you can't quite explain it!

Although many of my past life experiences bore some correlation, learning and understanding about my current life and what was going on in my everyday world, not all of them did.

One interesting one was a fairly simple and short life, where I had incarnated as a young Native American Indian girl. There was nothing particularly spectacular about the life itself, nor the death even. I had been walking alone through a wooded area and was happy skipping along, feeling the flowers with my hands as I moved forwards. In a second I was shot from behind and on my right hand side. Dead on the floor, I collapsed in a heap, hands over my wound, blood seeping through my slim brown fingers and feeling total shock at what had just taken place. I had had no prior inclination or warning I was even being watched. There was no sense of danger or that it was even a time of unrest.

The sense of shock and total confusion were very strong, "dirty bullet" were the words I used to describe the wound, there was no reason I could conceive for my being shot, for my life to be so cruelly taken. "I want to see myself old, I want to live the life I should have done. Old people die... I wasn't old."

It transpired that the energy of the spirit that was me in that lifetime as the Indian girl did not want to leave. The essence of that energy stayed with the body, then as the body was removed and burnt, the essence of her remained, clinging to the spot where her life was taken.

In our training we were taught to continue dialoguing with the person and the energy, to find out how long that energy stays there and ultimately what it needs to return to the light, its source, the place it belongs.

This is basically what some people might call the energy of a ghost, it is the essence of the energy of the person that has died and for whatever reason, the energy has found itself stuck or has chosen to stay close to places that hold some importance and meaning.

It was interesting for me to be seeing, sensing and feeling this about my own personal energy - even though that person was different to me as I am now, our core energy comes from and returns to a place that is amazing to encounter. Place is probably the wrong word as it is not a fixed location as such but when you tap into that essence of you, it is an energy that feels and tastes of you - it is your essence, regardless of how you may physically look. It feels of you, you at your best, you in your aspect of love and is your unique energetic vibration, that connects you to all things.

To me that higher vibration is your spirit, your higher self if you will. Some of that energy feeds the aspect of you that incarnates; this to me is the soul - it now has its own life and experiences, which all add to the flavour and texture, creating a slightly different essence, which when the body no longer has need of, that new essence and energy returns to the source, which continues to grow and evolve.

In my session, my guide was talking me through the shock, which was the overriding feeling I had as I entered that regression. After discovering there was not much of a story about the lifetime itself, I was guided to look at what the energy needed. Did I need to see the body, what was it that held me there? In answer to that I replied I wanted to see me get old, I didn't want to go.

Apparently I stayed there for many years; I was "tied to the place". And in literal, energetic terms, I was; I had indeed tied myself to that place. My utter shock and confusion had taken precedence over the natural flow of energy and the release of that spirit energy from the body.

I know such things are greatly written and talked about but what I found most helpful to me, personally was that I experienced this BEFORE I'd read anything about the possibility. In the regression, I instinctively knew what needed to be done with my energy; I knew why it was there, how it came about and where it needed to go, to make things feel right.

We spent more time in the realm of working with the energy of the spirit for that regression session, not the past life itself. I feel really comfortable there, it always has such an underlying current of love and support, compassion and understanding all the while you know you are privileged to be experiencing it and that you are working with the greater part of yourself. I hope that makes sense, as it is so hard at times to find the right words.

I needed reassurance from other souls, who had passed, people I felt safe with to be able to release my energy from that place and to reintegrate it. The willingness to leave and the realisation that it would be a safe transition were key elements for me to allow the process to take place, something which up until then I had blocked.

"They want me to go...my group... they reach out for me.. I sort of want to stay though..I'm scared to let go altogether."

Prompted to "go to a time when you move happily to the light... when you go home."

I was able to feel my energy moving on. I described it as if I were being pulled, pulled upwards and towards "Something I love, that feels good, even if I can't see it as such". The nearer I got, the better it felt. I also got a sense of me leaving that place and as I left I was ravelling back my energy as if I were almost winding a ball of wool - a golden thread of experience and information.

When asked what I needed to do with that energy right then, I wanted to hold it over my solar plexus area and it felt as if it melted into my system, as if it was returning home and strengthening me all at the same time.

My solar plexus, had been the place on my body, where I had felt the first sensations of that past life as one of the techniques we regularly used was to ask the question, where are you feeling that sensation in your body?

The body can hold memories, even if we are not consciously aware of them when we are in our every day mode of functioning and being. It is only when we tap into the subconscious that such things can become clear.

Knowing more about energy now, and the solar plexus area, I understand it is such a power house and why it felt so right to restore energy to that centre for me back then.

8 LIFE BETWEEN LIVES

One of my most memorable past life experiences was whilst I was training for my senior level hypnotherapy certification. We were a tiny group and we had time to indulge in detailed therapeutic sessions for each other and I was lucky to be sharing this with people who were very experienced in all sorts of psychic phenomena. If our sessions got slightly sidetracked by other, deeper subjects or healing we would work with those and incorporate them into whatever we were scheduled to be doing.

We had all experienced quite a lot of past life work thus far and it came up in conversation that it might be nice to do some life between life work. One of my colleagues was undergoing training to be able to guide such sessions and of course I was very willing to experience this. I wondered what it would be like, where do we go between lives, do we really make the decisions and then forget all about them as we incarnate? There was no way I was missing this opportunity.

The session began by taking me back to early years of my childhood in this life, things weren't necessarily flowing smoothly as I wasn't seeing or sensing much initially. The poor lady guiding me was wonderfully patient and was asking me questions about my childhood but I was already somewhere else. Although that somewhere else wasn't making much sense. Luckily she stopped asking about my childhood and then asked "What's going on for you now."

Great, that was it, I could describe what I was feeling, it seems that as I start to describe things I see more, and then the story unfolds, it's a bit like asking questions, until you start asking, you don't get answers - the trick seems to be in asking the right questions!

" I feel like I'm going somewhere, a definite feeling going through the length of me, a twisting inside... my body is buzzing.. feels like everything inside is tingly... like a rod"

"Can you describe the rod?"

"I can't see it but I can feel it."

"What does it feel like?"

"There is one area of heat."

"Can you describe what you sense?"

"Like a feeling of space..I'm everywhere but nowhere...I can feel my energy, but not anything else.."

At this point I was aware that this might not be the standard kind of session my companion had been hoping for but the feeling I had in my body was so real that I wanted to stay with it. Although I was in a mild trance state, I was not totally unaware of where I was and what was going on but I didn't want to pull myself out back to full waking consciousness. Luckily Betty, my companion didn't want to stop either; she had done a lot of psychic work and was keen to see where we went and what happened.

"Look down at yourself, describe the rod, is it going from front to back - or where to where?" Looking at this now, I would think that Betty was assuming that I had been struck by a spear or something and that I was probably describing having been garrotted. Neither of us were prepared for what I actually said.

"Round rock.. like having a volcano within, like a fire... as far as it goes in, it goes out...heat..fire..it's a natural process.."

"Can you be more specific?"

"Can see the rocks moving really fast.. it was part of something else...fire..."

Oh great - I was describing being a rock - a meteorite infact is how it transpired. I was tempted to leave this out but you know what - it happened, that's what I saw and felt and as I said before I'm not one for making stuff up. At the risk of sounding like a bit of a fruit loop I've included it. That is what I saw and felt.

As the session continued, I was aware of that meteorite, plummet to earth, of being below the surface of water, then there was a sense of being immersed in light. All the while my breathing rate had been deepening and slowing, so much so that Betty had made a note of it in her session notes.

I later described what I was feeling then as being 'plugged in'. I could feel energy coursing through my body, but it felt good, really good, I loved being able to tangibly experience something like that. My heart was pounding not with fear but a kind of excited anticipation. My fingers tingled, my knees felt as if there was a pressure inside them. I felt as if I were bigger somehow. My senses expanded and it was like being able to feel beyond your skin.

 I was sensing and seeing so much but couldn't find words at the time to describe it very well. Having to formulate words was hard work and took my focus away from enjoying what I was experiencing.

"Do you want to stay with that energy for a minute?"

I nodded and enjoyed the experience. It was like dissolving and somehow becoming whole at the same time, I was so pleased to be feeling this, even if I didn't know precisely what it was, it felt so, so good.

After a minute Betty asked "What's happening for you now?"

"I can feel energy through my body."

"Can you describe it at all?"

"Like the power of a heart beat."

"Are you still in the place of light you mentioned?"

"Yes."

The impression of being surrounded by light and energy then turned into me being in the centre of a room of light. I described what I thought was mirrors on the wall but as I got closer to look at them the mirrors were really pictures, moving pictures or scenes.

"I can see a mirror, I'm looking in the mirror...there are lots of people on the other side... they go back a long way... lots of them there...no I don't know them"

The first one I looked into was what I described as being a river of souls, people waving at me, as if they knew me but they weren't people I could recognise as such. It felt like they were thanking me, although I had no idea for what. That was on the wall in front of me - which wasn't a solid wall but a wall of light, from which I could just think of something and it would appear. Everything on that wall was the one colour, a golden vibrant shade, it was fluid-like almost, where shapes could be moulded and formed, they moved as if alive and changed as you looked at them.

On the wall to the right of me were 3 more mirror type pictures. I couldn't understand the images in these, one was a bird and a bear, there were the souls again and then an image of plants, which were growing out of the frame.

Betty questioned me on these and I answered that they weren't making much sense to me - I just described what I saw but felt something was missing, she prompted did I need someone else to come in and help me?

"I answered that questions felt like they were stopping things."

She paused for some time and then we continued as she again asked if I needed someone else there to help me make sense of things.

With that I was aware of another soul or spirit energy coming into the room from the doorway, which I hadn't noticed before, to the left and behind me. This was a male energy and he came straight to me, holding my hand, it was as if our energy merged. I was quiet for some time and did not respond to the questioning from Betty.

Finally I could speak; this was a very familiar energy to me, we had worked together before and loved each other before. Although in my daily 'normal' life I had not been aware of this. We had shared a strong connection in the past and would do so again. We were dancing for joy and immersed in love, it's like our hearts were bursting with celebration at being able to share this moment again. It was an amazing reunion and the sense of merging was like millions of tiny bubbles fizzing.

The energy felt like someone I knew, although at the time, we were only acquaintances. As it transpired two years later we were very much in love and people would often comment when we were in the same room, at how they could feel the energy between us, it was more than being in love. It was as if the excitement and bubbling we felt in our own energy systems could be felt by others too.

"You need to tell me what you're being told or shown so it can be recorded."

"Oh.. there's two of us..energy very similar...we're dancing..joy..unexpected help..for souls..dancing..going down to help... the pictures are all ready.. to integrate..all three.. others are her creation.. the other pictures... the other walls."

This didn't make much sense but the most important thing was the feeling, the experience. Not having had a near death experience as such I can't be sure but I would say this was very similar. It was a place of high energy and yet at the same time it was incredibly safe, buzzing with love and peace in the purest sense. Finding words to describe it is so hard as they limit it somehow. If you could bathe in the energy of the most beautiful music, feeling every cell in your body kissed by the reverberating tingle of sound, that might go some way to describing it.

We ended the regression without actually finding any life between life information. The session had been intense and had already been quite lengthy. We were both blown away by the strength of the energy we had felt and we left it as something I might want to work with again in the future. Betty was convinced it was a form of channelling and that at some point it might be relevant for me to revisit it.

.

9 FROZEN WITH FEAR

Experiencing a past life is usually pretty profound, even if it is for very different reasons. Some are energising, some are unravelling, some can bring up intense feelings and memories. One particular one, I remember, I was frozen with fear and cried and cried and cried....

What was interesting was how my mannerisms and language all corresponded with the age of the small child I was back then. My guide had to rephrase questions when they realised that I was responding as if I was a little girl.

The point at which I entered this past life, was not at the death point, it was a little before that. Having begun in the usual way, I was asked to concentrate on how my body was feeling and notice any sensations that weren't there when we started.

Almost immediately I'd moved my hands and arms up over my eyes,(even though I was already lying on the floor and had my eyes shut), and there they stayed for the majority of the session. I'd been so frightened and devastated by what I'd seen that my arms were there in the vain hope of shielding my eyes, so I wouldn't have to look anymore.

Initially I found it really hard to speak, I would just gently shake my head from side to side as if saying no...no...

The sadness and terror I felt were intense, it was as if I was frozen in a moment of time. At this point I had no inclination what it was I was unable to look at, all I was aware of was the numbness, disbelief and shock. This was the moment in that lifetime that held the most charge for me. It was intense shock and fear, in effect paralysing me.

"I just can't look.... I just can't look."

It was apparent to my tutor and guide that we were not going to be able to pursue this point just yet. When feelings or emotions are too strong, we will dissociate from that experience, get more understanding of the situation and then go back and face it later, finding out what the person needs to be able to go through the event.

I was asked to go back a little and explain what was going on, prior to this event that I found too painful to look at.

The tension subsided and I could now see a very different scene and was able to talk much more freely.

I was a young girl, 4 years old, dressed in an off white smock dress. It was a lovely day, about mid morning in late summer and I wanted to play. We lived in a very small hamlet, it was a simple life and the elders were busy as were most of the older children. I skipped my way to the edge of the meadow, where there was a raised mound, which acted as a boundary and was the place a watcher would sit. Their job was to keep an eye out for approaching travellers as trouble could descend on us very quickly, if we were not warned. It felt that although we were a peaceful community the times we lived in and the greater world were not so peaceful.

The job of watcher on this particular day had fallen to a young boy, less than ten years old; my brother. I pestered him and pestered him to come and play, to take me to the nearby lake. Initially he refused and we sat there for a while, laughing and playing, gently pushing each other and rolling down the bank. After a while I asked again if we could go paddling, couldn't he just take me there, just for a short while? I'd be really good and keep out of his way after that.

Eventually he relented and off we went. It must have been quite some distance, as we were gone for a good part of the day; it was afternoon before we approached home. He must have sensed something was wrong, or that he would be in trouble for having left his post. He stopped walking, suddenly alert. He turned to me, pushed me backwards and told me to stay there, to stay hidden. With that he was gone, running towards home.

I did as I was told and sat there for a while, then I got bored and a little bit scared in case I would be in trouble. I waited a little bit more and then decided to just walk home.

Asked to move on to the next 'significant event' at the count of three I was back where we started. The feelings were back just as strongly and my arms were back covering my eyes. This time though, I could slowly describe a bit more of what I was seeing, after I was reminded that this was not actually happening right now, but it required a great deal of patience from my guide.

I said I was standing in front of what had been our home. The scene I described and saw was one of complete carnage.

Huts were smouldering, dilapidated, broken; posts and railings were snapped like twigs. Fires were burning, cooking pots were knocked over, a few animals ran loose. But worst of all there were bodies, bodies and bits of bodies scattered and dropped to the floor where they had been slaughtered. Nobody had been left alive.

For a while the images were fuzzy as if coming into focus and I was gently prompted to move my hands away from my face, so that I could get a better look.

As I moved my hands away, I saw friends and family, bashed, bruised and broken. Stepping unsteadily closer I saw my mother in that lifetime, prostrate on the floor, well part of her anyway.

She'd been holding my baby sister... both were now a bloodied mess. Her eyes were open, as if they were looking at me, her red long hair stuck with dirt and blood. It made me feel physically sick and weakened at the knee. It was really hard for me to talk about and to describe. Although I was quite quiet, the silent tears I cried were intense and deeply felt. This was all my fault.

No one had been left alive, every single man, woman and child had been struck down, every building burnt or wrecked. Wild men on horses had come through and destroyed our lives in a very short space of time.

The next thing I recalled some time later was stumbling dazed on the one path through the settlement, coming through to the other side and there laid out face flat in the dirt was my older brother. Struck from behind, also broken, unceremoniously left where he fell.

This was a terrible story to relive and feel, to observe and to feel part of. The sense of devastation, loss, confusion and blame, all in a tiny 4 year old girl, with no real comprehension as to what, why or how it had happened.

Suddenly my heart started beating faster, faster, my guide could tell something was happening; it was as if every nerve and fibre in my body was tingling, not with excitement but abject fear. Something was coming. Someone was coming.

I could feel the drumming of horses hooves. Without looking behind I started to run, I didn't know why or where. I ran as fast and as hard as my little legs would go. Fear and panic driving me forward, I could feel the palpitations in my body as I was describing the scene to those listening.

Then there was nothing. It was gone.

Realising I had diverted and dissociated and knowing that this often occurs at vital points the person guiding my regression wanted to check those last few moments, to see what had happened.

Guiding me back to a few moments before the point of death, as if now watching the scene, I let it unfold as if I was viewing the scene rather than reliving it.

Indeed, I was running, running for my tiny life. A man on horseback was riding towards me. His fellow horsemen had done the damage, he was the last of them, bringing up the rear, and his only purpose was to make sure no one was left alive.

In a few strides he was upon me, his arm raised and a mace like weapon in his left hand. The spiked ball as I described it, hit me square in the back, lifting me up with the force of it and then dropping me down limp like a broken rag doll. The man rode on without the slightest remorse not even thinking about glancing back.

What was interesting to see from this perspective was the fact that seconds before the mace struck, my spirit left the body. I watched it happen. I watched the child run and saw the attack and also saw the golden energy rise up and leave the body. So there was no sense of pain, it was a welcome release from the terrible, intense fear.

As you can imagine there was some considerable time spent in the realm of spirit and energy to get some closure and understanding around this experience.

I needed to meet with all the relevant family members as well as the perpetrators and then wanted to bring in some much needed healing.

The horseman who delivered the deadly blow was known to me in this life and meeting his spirit in the afterlife was strange and we needed other guides to be brought in to help with the understanding and release. I was too frightened to meet him on my own. When asked who or what I needed to be with me, I'd wanted my dog, my mother and an angelic presence to be there, before I was able to allow his energy to draw near.

After some time and asking questions and waiting for answers it was described to me that he was "not of right mind". Although this was neither a reason nor an excuse, it did offer a chance for understanding. It had a touch of inevitability about it, there was nothing that could be done or said to undo that. It wasn't personal as such.

I wanted to meet with my brother of that lifetime to ask for his forgiveness as well as my mother, father and other brothers and sisters. I had felt it was my fault for pulling my brother away whilst he should have been on watch. I felt a lot of guilt and shame about it, which needed to be addressed.

Although I was convinced it was my fault as I had persuaded my brother to leave his post, it was shown to me that he simply would have been killed first not last. They were deadly quick and swift it was going to happen anyway. They were powerful men on sturdy horses; their only aim was to kill.

Obviously there was no direct comparison as such with my current life but I could relate to the fact of not wanting to see. I could understand that there were things going on around me that I was accepting on many levels as I was choosing not to see them to some degree or another. The not wanting to see didn't stop it from existing or happening. I was putting my head down and accepting some rough treatment from people around me that I would never expect anyone else to accept.

Even if I couldn't find words for it as such, just as that young girl couldn't find the words, my inner sense of integrity and morality, my honour knew that I did not deserve such things. And although change might seem scary, by choosing not to see the reality of what was going on, I was by default, accepting it not only for myself but for my children too.

10 OFF WITH THE FAIRIES!

One experience I had during a regression session had very little to do with a past life as such. Although everything had started in the normal manner I was neither getting a sense of a place nor a life event. Whilst lying down I'd changed position gradually as the trance state was deepened by my guide. I'd drawn my right hand over my chest and in the process clenched my fist loosely and twisted the hand as it rested at the base of my throat. My right shoulder had also been drawn in.

I was aware of sensations in my body, I described it as feeling stiff, almost dead to my right side but I was not seeing myself as a person. Instead the impression I got was of being an old gnarled tree, the branches twisted over. It also felt like the tree was shrouded in what I can only call a restrictive cobweb, I could feel it but it wasn't visible to the human eye.

This is where regression can be so interesting, you may start off looking for a life but anything that comes up, is there for a reason, a purpose and we tend to investigate it, to see if there is indeed a message or meaning of some kind to the person involved.

As it was still a light level of trance, I remember thinking why can't I just see what everyone else sees, they get lovely images of spirit guides; the native American chief, the wizened old man or a beautiful guru of some kind. What do I get - meteorites, rocks, fairies and trees!

Still, I knew it was real and that I actually preferred this kind of thing as I knew it wasn't me wanting to see specific images and to be honest I probably wouldn't have believed them if they had shown up! The images and sensations I saw and felt were always perfectly aligned with me. It was never the visual images that amazed me so much as the very real and tangible feelings I felt moving throughout my body. The moment I felt anything, I almost relaxed into the process even more as I knew it was nothing to do with my conscious mind. It's as if your ego takes a step to the side, all the pomp, pride and expectations it desperately clings on to shift out of the way, so the truth of the subconscious can reveal itself.

Anyway, there I was, symbolised as a tree, with twisted branches, surrounded by something that was keeping me stuck and restricted. As I was asked to concentrate on the feeling, I noticed a small fairy hovering around me. I was so hesitant at saying anything because it sounded so corny but there she was. She was removing and unravelling the fine cobwebby mist that surrounded the tree.

Looking back now, I would say that it symbolised a form of psychic attack, which at that time of my life would have been no doubt a reality. Some of the restriction was due to thought forms and much of it was kept in place by my own fearful thoughts at the time.

The fairy wound round and round me, unwinding and removing the cobweb and binds. My fellow trainee, acting as my guide on this occasion was very patient as it took a while, you can't do regression on the run! As the cobweb net was removed, the branches were able to move, what I hadn't noticed was that the tree had not been wholly devoid of life, there was life still running through the core and the left hand side was relatively unscathed, it was the right side that had been twisted and bent over.

Since that time having studied more about energy and metaphysics I understand that amongst other things, the right hand side of the body is to do with our male energy and attributes. Things like our ability to be proactive, take action, to assert ourselves and take charge.

At the time of my training I was attempting to leave a very controlling and domineering relationship. I might have had the desire for change but I was not taking purposeful action, consequently I was stuck.

This releasing and in effect the returning of my energy was very significant for me. I was able to finally stand up and say NO to what was going on. To realise I had the strength to make changes and that I not only deserved better but it was my right to be free.

11 THERE'S ALWAYS A WITCH

In this next lifetime, I entered the story suffocating inside a dark space, finding it hard to swallow and talk. The sense of suffocation was so strong. To understand more of the story, I was again guided back in time a little, to a calmer scene to start to pick up the threads of the story.

I was an elderly woman in the woods, slightly bent over, worn clothes and I was really aware of my old fingers and hands. Although not a witch as such, I did use herbs and plants from the surrounding area to live by and heal when I could. I lived a solitary and simple life and didn't engage much with the villagers that lived nearby.

My hands were twisted and misshapen, I described them as bumpy and sore and it was one of the reasons I kept my distance from the others as they thought they had a chance of catching whatever it was I had. My knuckles were swollen and very obvious and it was better to avoid the harsh comments and recriminations of the local people.

One day out foraging, I'd come across a small child, a young girl. She seemed to have fallen and hit her head. She was not moving but I could tell she was still alive. I'd looked around and found no one else and decided the best thing to do was to take her back to my shelter.

This I did and then fixed her wound as best I could. I was uncomfortable having a stranger in my home but I couldn't leave her outside. As evening was almost upon us, I thought I'd leave her to rest and hope she would be better in the morning, so either she could go back home or I could go and take her back to the village.

Things turned out a little differently however.

Early the next morning, I heard the noise of people approaching, people shouting as they came closer. I went to open the door as a man in his forties pushed hard on the door. He was so angry. I fell back as the edge of the door struck me.

Quickly followed by others, he barged into my hovel and saw the girl, lying prostrate. In less than a second the throng erupted with a mass of verbal accusations and shouts. They assumed I had taken her and she was there against her will and that I was obviously up to no good. I had neither the wit nor the strength to appeal. I attempted to step forward, stretching out my hands, attempting to show them her wound. I was scared and ineffective.

They shouted and moved away from my outstretched hands. One of them picked up the child and bundled her away.

The man, her father picked up a log by the fire and struck out and hit me with it, sending me flying, I hit the table and slumped to the floor, now unconscious myself.

There was a scuffle as the men, kicking at the simple sticks of wood which made up my furniture were overtaken by anger and wrath. The table was overturned as they left and it had fallen on top of me.

It didn't finish there for me though; the smouldering embers of the logs that were now kicked all about the floor began to take light. They created a lot of smoke which was filling my lungs as I lay there on the edge of consciousness; dazed, confused and dying.

This was only a snippet of a lifetime and looking at it now, even so, I would say that there are psychological similarities for me in that story. Time was spent as usual, bringing in healing and gaining insight regarding the greater perspective and what that might mean to me.

Revisiting these past life experiences causes me to again consider the meaning and implications to a greater degree than I did at the time. Just as when we first read a book, when we go back and read it some time later, we get something else from it that we didn't initially see.

12 THE THERAPEUTIC PESPECTIVE

So far I have shared with you some of my own personal regression experiences and from this point, these stories are chiefly those belonging to clients.

Alongside their story I've included comments about the process, the purpose and the outcome, where appropriate, in the hope that it will provide a more complete picture. I've used the basic structure of a typical regression session to provide the outline for the next few chapters. Taking you from the initial interview to the point of integration.

- Interview
- Method of Entry; The Bridge
- The Character
- The Story; Diversions & Dissociations
- The Death Point
- The Afterlife
- Integration

13 THE INTERVIEW

Having ascertained that regression is suitable for the client and an experience that they wish to undertake we spend time talking about their symptoms or experiences that have brought them to this point. We might talk about the number of times something has happened or the feelings surrounding an event. The terms they use to describe things can be very enlightening for example and will often provide keys to starting to unlock the memories and give us relevant triggers.

With a clear idea of the client's history we also ascertain the other people involved, and the outcome the client would like. It's important that the client feels safe and comfortable disclosing what is very personal, sometimes even embarrassing and painful information. It's important they are free to disclose whatever it is they see and/ or feel without recrimination or judgement.

Our past lives can be very colourful and there will undoubtedly be instances of trauma of one kind or another. Alongside the events will be a variety of associated feelings; fear, guilt, shame etc. We as therapists have to be prepared for anything as there is no telling what might come up during the sessions. If the client feels an element of distrust or doesn't feel completely safe, then they are hardly likely to feel free to share, if important elements are left uncovered or 'politely smoothed over' then the healing will probably only be partial.

We came across this quite a bit when we were training as a group as it can be hard enough to share personal information on a one to one basis but when you have several people around you, watching and listening it can be quite disconcerting.

One of the men in the group just couldn't get to the place where he felt comfortable enough to relax into the process. He would start trial sessions with good intentions but something in him strongly resisted going past a certain point. As soon as he started to remember feelings of fear he would bring himself back and break the connection. He admitted to feeling that he was not sure he actually wanted to experience regression; he acknowledged he was "filled with too many doubts, too much fear and cynicism".

It made him uncomfortable and he didn't feel he was in a place to pursue that or push his boundaries. He liked the idea of the process but was not ready to experience it fully himself and consequently he left the course, hoping to be able to pick it up again in a few years. He was going through some life changes at the time which left him emotionally raw and exhausted, the intellectual aspect of learning a new skill had appealed to him but the level of personal experience of regression required was too much for him at that time.

14 THE POINT OF ENTRY

When we are ready to begin the regression itself, we use a variety of 'bridging techniques'; these literally take us from one place to another. These bridges might be verbal, emotional or physical, we could use hypnosis or even free association. I personally preferred the physical or emotional variety to use as access points, both for myself and my clients.

In my own first regression, I was skilfully led into the experience by describing my emotions. The discovery of my husband's affair literally had knocked the wind out of me; I'd gone weak at the knees and had had to hold on to something to stop myself from collapsing. I was asked a few questions about the sensations I felt, and where I felt them most in my body.

"My stomach.... it's churning and churning, I feel weak... shocked....sickened... right to the core.."

Then I was asked to go back to the first time I had felt those feelings.

That was it, the sensations seemed to get stronger, this is when I started to move, feeling as though I was collapsing at my centre, holding my stomach, rhythmically contracting into myself.

This had only taken what felt like seconds, from simply explaining my feelings from a current life event I had stepped across into the experience of that previous life.

As it was near the beginning of the session, I was not deeply embedded in the character or story and my conscious, rational mind was busy trying to make sense of what was happening. But I didn't want to pull myself back out of it - I knew I was really feeling what I was feeling, I knew I wasn't being hurt at that specific moment but I was also aware that my body was moving as if it was. I had no actual pain but the memory was vivid and my body was definitely reliving something. I suppose it's a bit like watching a film, where we flinch when the character is being hit on screen.

This is often the point we can most easily stop the process and it is necessary to use other techniques to 'embody the character' more. However if a session starts with such an obvious physical or emotional reaction, we let it play out and we will make sense of it and find out further details as the intensity subsides.

I remember being surprised at the way I was moving and just how real it felt. As I mentioned earlier I am not one for overt expression or dramatic episodes and certainly at that particular point in my life I was pretty shy and quiet. But alongside the surprise was a feeling of relief and pleasure, I knew with every cell in my body that this was going to be good for me and that by knowing I was not consciously making these movements, they had completely taken me by surprise then something was going on that probably needed to happen and the best thing I could do was to get out of my own way and let it unfold.

For me, personally this was the best technique without doubt, as my conscious mind had been totally bypassed, if a bridge using free association for example had been used, I probably would have just thought I was making it all up. By awakening the memories stored in my body, my first experience of regression was visceral and pretty intense, totally catching my brain off guard.

All in a few seconds, I was shocked, pleased, intrigued and eager to know what would happen next.

Which technique to use is a choice the therapist makes once they have spoken with the client. They may have personal favourites yet when the situation arises to deviate they will do that as it's always useful to have a few different approaches.

The verbal bridge involves using the client's language; they may use specific terms or phrases to describe their situation, even a certain vocal tone. This is especially useful if they marry their words with a specific movement, expression or hand gesture for example. Getting them to repeat the phrase can be very useful and it can bring up related emotions and memories. From there we might ask about the images that come up for them as they say the words over and over and suddenly we can both find we are on that bridge to a previous life.

The same goes for the physical bridge, here the client might talk of a bodily symptom, either a chronic condition or one that doesn't seem to make any sense. For example they may feel choking type sensations, without any real physical reason for doing so, they may have joint or muscle problems that do not appear to have a cause or answer in their current life. Here we might ask questions about what the sensation feels like, is it heavy, numb or sharp? Asking them to describe it more and almost go into it is another way of accessing the deeper story behind it.

Helping us across the bridge and further into the past life we might use the term 'as if'. We might repeat the sensation the client has noticed and then ask them to finish the sentence with as if....The purpose here is to get more information and to continue the initial exploratory process, for with every new detail the level of experience is deepening.

A client might say they have a stinging sensation in their right shoulder;

Therapist: "Focus on that stinging sensation in your shoulder, and finish the sentence.. it's as if...."

Client " yes, the stinging... it's burning... it's as if ....I've been stabbed"

The client is usually by this stage grimacing or making movements that correspond with someone having been stabbed. This is the point where disorientation and confusion can sneak in as the client is obviously aware they are lying on a couch speaking to the therapist yet feeling physical sensations without the actual pain. This is a point where we can consciously decide it feels too much as it can be a bit scary and certainly unusual to experience the two things at once.

Hence the need for trust in your therapist as you need to feel safe enough to relax as well as feel confident in their ability to guide you sensitively, even if things feel a little bizarre or strange, knowing they have your best interests at all times.

The Physical Bridge

Often we enter a past life at or near the death point as in the example of the stabbing above. We might also enter at a very peaceful point. Using the method of scanning the body energy, allows us to use any noticeable change in physical sensations the client may have.

Helen for instance reported feeling a pressure just above her knees, when asked to describe what that pressure related to, using the 'it's as if' expansion she answered:

" Oh.. it's as if I'm leaning against a gate.. yes a gate.. I am overlooking a field, leaning against the bars of the gate...it's a lovely sunny day and I feel warm... I'm waiting.. waiting for something.. someone."

Being sensitive to energy I favoured the body scan method, with the client comfortable, usually laying down feeling relaxed and at ease, I would simply ask them to pay attention to the feelings and sensations in their body, noticing any symptoms that didn't seem to be there previously.

I would then set my intention to be looking for any past life residues or instances that were appropriate for us to uncover and work with. (Whatever level of energy work is undertaken, we always check we have permission to work with it and release it). Then I would simply run my hands a few inches above their body, telling them the areas I was hovering over as they usually had their eyes closed. I would feel a sensation in my own hands and energy, sensing where the energy felt different. Without me having to say anything the client would usually nod their head to acknowledge yes, something did indeed feel different and they were now aware of a sensation that they hadn't noticed before.

Jason started to feel something straight away, initially it was

"...heat in the ears and a bit dizzy in the head... and oh.. yeh my right shoulder, it's throbbing.... as if .. oh.. a small child being pulled by the shoulder"

"Who's pulling?"

"Other people.. jostling...we're outside, there's a cobbled street.. it's grey, dismal, drizzly, I've got bare legs, my trousers are just below the knee.. he's dragging me along.. I'm about 6 or 7.. I don't want to go.. he's angry.. so angry.. it's my father."

Jason went on to describe being frightened of his father, yet respecting him and knowing no different, it was an accepted lot in life. They were a poor family and his father had been a strict and serious man. As we moved the story along he recalled waiting at a fishing wharf, waiting and waiting. His mother had died when he was a toddler and he had been told to wait there for his father to return.

Although the day faded into dusk, he daren't move, he had been told to wait and wait he would. He crouched for warmth and shelter from the wind by some crates. Eventually ladies with shawls, talking and laughing came by and "..they take me away from that place..he won't be coming back.. we go into a dark passageway, and a building, they give me something to eat" exhausted he fell asleep.

He lived out several years in that place, basically living as a servant, realising eventually that this was a house of ill repute. He could hear the ladies laughing and remembered taking the coats from the many gentlemen visitors. Moving further into the life, he described being married;

"I finally have something... a family.. my lady and a little boy..." The realisation and images he had of the small boy brought tears to his eyes and softened his heart.

"We're in the park, it's a nice day.. I'm not in that house anymore... I have something.. something good.. finally.. it feels good.. different to before.. this is what happy feels like.." And once again gentle tears were streaming from his eyes with the warmth of the memory.

As our job is to guide the story, I encouraged Jason to move to the next significant event and then everything went dark and he could see no more. This is a diversion and often means this might be an area worth pursuing.

Guiding him back to that lifetime, and to a relevant point he recalled;

"I'm in a boat, something is wrong.. with the boat..oh god.. other people are here as well but I don't know them.. I feel afraid.. I'm not going back.." The realisation that he was watching his own death and the thought of leaving behind the woman he loved and his child he adored, the happiness he had only just been blessed to feel, again brought tears. This time they were much more painful and deeper.

As the tears subsided he continued.." The sea's rough.. they're panicking.. water is coming in.. over the sides.. it's tipping.."

With a sharp intake of breath he went on " Oh.. the water.. it's *so* cold .. it's going over, it's on top, hang on to something.. struggle.. I can't swim.. trying to breathe.. I don't want to go.. I can't... not now...it's going in my mouth.. I can't see.. I can't breathe...it's all black."

Jason was quiet for some time and I didn't interrupt as I could see from his facial expressions and body language and the energy he was giving off that a lot was going on for him. As things calmed down a little I asked to check that the heart had stopped beating in that lifetime.

"Yes.... awful, awful sadness, heart breaking loss... the child.. the little boy.. so sad... and for the lady.... I didn't want to go... not fair... I was finally happy."

Once the emotions had once again settled a little, we worked on bringing a sense of peace and understanding by viewing that lifetime from the perspective of the spirit world, the afterlife.

Here we met all the relevant characters from that life, his mother, his father, getting an understanding about their lives and how things came to be the way they were. We met the ladies who had taken him in and of course we reunited him with the spirits of his wife and his son.

This aspect of working with the afterlife, the spirits and souls of personalities involved in the story of each lifetime is a beautiful thing. It is humbling and inspiring at the same time. To work with the fabric of love that creates life and unites us all expands the heart in a way that is hard to describe with words and it touches you in such a way that you never quite view life in the same way again.

Using Hypnosis

Although using hypnosis as a means to enter a past life is not usually my method of choice, I was working with a client, Jackie for a phobia she had. She'd had one session with me previously to introduce her to what hypnosis felt like and to encourage her to relax.

Jackie was 52 years old, happily married with no children. She was a company secretary, enjoyed her work and was very analytical. Although her general health was good, she did find it difficult to relax. The reason she had come to me for hypnosis though, was to tackle her irrational fear of heights.

She was quite annoyed at herself about it, as it didn't make sense to her at all. She liked to sit in the window seat of an aeroplane and yet would never use a multi storey car park, or a ladder. She also would only ever stay on the ground floor in hotels wherever possible and if she had to have a higher room she kept the curtains closed.

This had been getting progressively worse over the past ten years and she was now fed up with it. This fear was affecting her life too much now for her to ignore it. She was adamant that things must change, she was going to America in 3 months time, to celebrate her 25th wedding anniversary and she had set herself a goal of going to the top of the Empire State Building!

She had decided that she would try hypnotherapy. Our first session was more talking than anything else and as Jackie was quite anxious I told her we wouldn't tackle the issue today at all but what we would do is induce a state of relaxation, which I would record for her. She was to take that recording home and listen to it for the next week until we met again.

One week later she returned, reporting she had never slept so well at night and that she was really looking forward to continuing. Having established that she responded well to hypnosis we began the next session with the view to tackling her phobia.

Neither of us at that point had envisaged the root cause would lie in a past life memory. Having started with the simple induction she was already used to, to create the appropriate level of relaxation I then used a standard technique of taking Jackie down a set of stairs and with each step down she would feel more and more relaxed. At the bottom of the stairs was a special corridor, a corridor with many doors, she was to choose the door that held the answer for her current phobia and fear of heights.

Turning the handle and stepping inside we entered into a past life.

Jackie recalled being a little girl, playing in an apple tree, there was no great fear or other underlying issue with that lifetime. She had fallen from the tree, had been hurt and nobody else was near enough to help. The consequence being she died on the ground, alone, hurt and scared. Rather than move on, her spirit had stayed stuck with the body and had even lingered for years after, effectively attached to the spot.

To enable the spirit to move on, having established what she felt she needed, we called in the energy of her mother in that lifetime, there was a tearful reunion and with her mother by her side, the energy of the spirit of that little girl was able to move on. In effect she was able to find peace. We checked there was no unfinished business left with that lifetime.

The energy from that small spirit had been causing a disturbance or resonance in Jackie's energy; one that she could not have understood without visiting that previous life. She had no cause for the fear from this lifetime and it didn't seem to make much sense at all nor fit in with her own personality of this current life.

Jackie was delighted to have found a cause, a reason and to have seen and dealt with it. It had been an emotional journey but in a good sense.

As we tied up the session, we established that she would tackle some real world heights in measurable doses over the next week, starting with a step ladder in the kitchen and then a multi storey car park at the weekend.

Our third and final session embedded her success thus far and the positive outcome she wanted of going up the Empire State Building.

We were both ecstatic when she called me from the 86th floor about a fortnight later and it is something neither of us will ever forget.

15 BREATHING LIFE INTO THE MEMORIES

The techniques I've touched on so far serve to get the momentum of the past life going, they are the initial entry point, opening a doorway that has long been closed. To move things on and to help establish the scene we as therapists, simply ask questions which cause the client to look a little deeper. As they provide us with the answers, they are naturally sinking into the experience more, without having to try or force anything.

The questions can be as simple as:

- What are you wearing?
- Are you male or female?

- Look down at your feet, what do you see?
- Are there other people around you?

They may see shoes or sense they are bare foot. If the client can't get a clear sense of clothing, we might ask about body areas, are you wearing anything on your head? Do you get a sense of clothes, are your arms covered, if so what does the material feel like.. is it soft or scratchy? And so it goes on. Bringing their attention to detail helps them to embody the character and to establish the scene they find themselves in.

To describe it, I would say it's a bit like watching a dream to begin with and then all of a sudden it hits you that it's you you're watching. The person feels like you and is you, even though it may not look like you in this life time and may even be a different sex to what you are now. There is no doubt in your mind you are watching yourself, the watching soon becomes experiencing as the story progresses and as you answer these simple questions.

Sheila was describing finding herself, in a mountainous area, she looked down and saw "...white socks.. and there's embroidery here" as she pointed to her chest " and puffy sleeves, they go all the way down to my wrists..Moccasins on my feet... I'm a man."

She continued on to experience a landslide, with herself and many of her friends caught up in the devastation. There was a lot of fear and panic involved and she was very anxious about protecting her energy in this life. She was interested in healing and yet was scared about what she might be dealing with at the same time. Consequently she found she was attracting a lot of negative energy, that seemed to cause her to feel that the ground was being pulled from under her and things were out of her control.

Experiencing the past life helped her to make correlations with her current life. Energy work, both the protective kind and the kind involving dealing with intrusive energies was the route we took to help Sheila. These are not necessarily part of regression work but they often sit alongside it as they all live within our subtle energy fields.

16 WELCOME CATHARSIS

To me catharsis is more than just an emotional release; it feels like it includes a level of understanding and appreciation with it. In this sense the word describes a healing physically taking place and that can be on many levels; physically, mentally, emotionally and spiritually. As such the client can be left feeling quite exhausted by what they have experienced as what has been experienced is at quite a deep and profound level.

On occasion during the regression we might use various techniques to guide the process, to check we have all the facts, that we've met all the relevant people, we've travelled back and forth in time possibly several times in order to do this. It's not a therapy that can be done in a hurry and requires great patience.

One of the most powerful techniques can be the use of simple props or using psychodrama to heighten an experience when it feels right. This can be particularly useful for people who are very kinaesthetic in nature, responding to touch and visceral experiences.

Patricia had been regressed back to a life in Greece, as a man in that lifetime she had been apprehended by "The blue caps" for smuggling secrets of some kind. She'd avoided capture as the boat she was travelling in moored in a cave and she'd then scrabbled along dusty tunnels, arriving in the back room of a simple tavern type building.

Other people were there and she'd attempted to mingle with the crowd, keeping her head down. Unfortunately she was captured, smothered in a cloth which was then tied and bound around her, so she felt as if she was in a sack of some kind. Feeling frightened, unable to see, with the dirt and dust of the cloth closing in around her, feeling the heat and restriction of being bound up this way.

All of a sudden she would dissociate from this experience; the level of discomfort seemed to get too much and she would suddenly recall a previous lighter aspect of that life. After allowing this to happen a few times and persistently going back, bit by bit she was able to let more of the story unfold. She died beaten and bruised in that sack, aware of her consciousness slipping in and out, not being able to see, breathe or fight back, feeling helpless and useless.

Once all the story was gathered and experienced and after some work in the spirit realm, she described still feeling uncomfortable about being covered and it felt to her like that it was necessary to do some more work. Interestingly in her initial interview she had mentioned she occasionally suffered with asthma type attacks and the feeling of not being able to breathe. She also later confided that she couldn't stand her head to be covered by the bed clothes and often felt anxious at night. After some discussion we agreed we would do some work to help relieve this feeling, she wanted to be able to physically do something about it. Telling her before hand what I would do so she would not be unduly alarmed or shocked we used simple props.

We returned to the time where she was feeling bound, helpless and unable to breathe. I gently placed a towel on top of her representing the feeling of the sack. She was able to now grab at it, and pull it away, in effect freeing herself from her previous state of futility.

This is so simple in our waking state, yet in the regressed, almost hypnotic trance like state using such props is immensely powerful, we can use them to increase tension and intensity or to break the binds that tie us. To the client and the subconscious mind there is no difference between the towel and the sack, but the ability to do something about the situation can bring a release on many levels.

We often use this technique in a loving sense. In the spirit world as we meet our loved ones, often estranged or having been distant for long periods of time, the client wants to hug their mother, father, son or daughter. As we invite them to let them draw close we will pass them a cushion, a tangible something to draw their arms around and hold close. This is so powerful and often evokes such tears and can be one of the most touching moments of the entire experience.

17 AT THE POINT OF DEATH

One of the key areas in a past life experience is obviously the death point. Not just because it's the moment we died but because the dying thoughts, emotions, beliefs and feelings are what we take with us into the afterlife.

Things left unresolved and unfinished, whether real or misunderstood carry a resonance, an energy with them and it is this very energy that can ripple with us in future lives. It is usually this unfinished business that has rippled in our current lives, prompting us to seek regression, even if it is as a last resort having tried just about everything else we can think of.

If the energy of the soul stays lost or around the body at the time of death and doesn't move on to the greater realm of light and peace we might notice feeling stuck or lacking energy of some kind in this lifetime. This is very much how we might understand the energy of lost souls or ghosts.

Hannah shared her memories of a previous life as a soldier, seeing her friends die in battle, unceremoniously, feeling a nervous kind of adrenaline. When the time came for her own death, she didn't want to go;

" I don't deserve this.. I don't want to go.. why should I go.. I'm so angry.."

It transpired she was so reluctant to leave that life and body that a small piece of her energy stayed. When asked what that piece represented she immediately replied "Fear!.. Fear of change."

She didn't like not knowing what was coming next and wanted to stay with what she knew, stay in the same place, "Stay where it finished."

In the afterlife she realised she had forgotten this had been part of her own plan; " I forgot.. that I planned it... God it makes so much sense now."

She felt that she needed to bring in added courage, to fill the void that she felt had been created in her energy. When asked about any correlations with this life, she spoke very candidly;

"Fear of the unknown I suppose.. I do, I stick with what I know, the same old thing, not wanting to move on.

I always think other people know more than I do, I never know enough, yet inside I know I know enough. It's like I fight with myself - I know I should move on but feel unable to do so a lot of the time.

What have I learnt? Right now - well - that I do have the answers, they're MY answers, and it's OK to move. There's no real safety in trying to keep things the same."

Similarly dying thoughts of hopelessness and futility, such as with Patricia, dying bound in a sack can carry forward and might be recognised in bouts of depression or feelings of helplessness in this life for example.

In fact Patricia had several lives where she'd died with similar feelings and thoughts. She recalled being a dark skinned slave, in chains, left to starve and fester in her own detritus. There was a recognisable theme of having no choice, no hope, lives of depravity, sad and meagre existences.

She saw a correlation in her attitude to just give up, to not apply much ambition or energy to things, "I almost give up before I've even started." Her anxiety and asthma meant she wouldn't physically exert herself too much, she felt she had little or no will power. After a few such lives, she grew tired of the theme, seeing it as a chance to change now or accept the same for this life.

In one of the afterlife sessions, I asked if she would meet with her own higher self, the beautiful spirit energy version of herself to see what help and advice they might have.

In effect this was like meeting herself as her own best friend, one that knew only love for her, appreciating her journey and seeing her authentic self. Meeting this aspect of her, touching her spirit as I like to call it, was a beautiful experience for her. To touch that level of love and understanding is a gift and it is one we are all capable of. She was able to start to make positive changes in her life and her attitude, seeing how she was creating situations in this life that were modern replicas of what she had experienced before. Seeing the bigger picture she now wanted life to be different and consequently decided she would be more proactive in making things happen.

18 THE AFTERLIFE

When we use our past life experiences as a therapy, we spend a lot of time in the spirit world or afterlife. For it is here that we can gain a better and more compassionate understanding of each lifetime. Not only that, for we can meet with other souls and bring in the things we feel we need for healing, help or understanding. We can replay past events, not to pretend that they didn't happen but to bring a sense of peace and harmony. It is also here we can release pent up feelings, energy and emotion and the forgiveness we both give and receive here is deeply felt.

Bethany had entered a past life at a particularly gruesome point, saying she had a bizarre sensation in her neck, throat and chest and very quickly that was followed by "It's all red.. oh my God... my head is not there!" Going with what presents itself first, the death point was fully explored as was the entire life story.

She had a loving husband and they lived a rural, country life. She used the natural medicine of the herbs and plants she foraged, not just to cook with but to heal and make simple tinctures and the like.

She was mistrusted by the other villagers and at a time of mass fear and hysteria, she had been beheaded as it was their belief that was the only way to make sure the witch could not come back to cause them harm. She saw the guillotine and recalled the intense fear, humiliation, anger and sense of loss she felt.

Her spirit had been able to leave her body but she had not wanted to leave her children in that lifetime behind; she stayed earthbound to watch them grow old.

In the realm of the spirit world she was able to not only reunite with her beloved children and family, she was also able to meet the villagers to let them see she had never been any threat to them. They were able to release their guilt and shame, and she could let go of her shock, anger and disbelief.

What she most wanted to do though, was to give her dying body the dignity of being restored; she wanted to place her head back with her body. She went to the place where she could see both her head and her body and gently placed the two back together so she could see herself whole and healed. She wanted to do this with her family and the villagers watching. It was important to her that they observed her restoring her power and dignity. As they all watched she felt the shame she had carried seeping away. It was as if her power and lightness of spirit were being returned to her. She had a sense of being restored with a fabulous current of love and compassion, not just for herself but for all of those who had been involved.

After some time as the villagers saw the error of their ways they explained to her how the current of fear had overtaken any rational thoughts and ways of being from them. She was able to check that there was no more unfinished business and that she was able to now move away with a sense of peace and completion.

A similar experience was described by Paula. She entered the life with a strong sense of failure and not being able to control things. She repeated several times a phrase she had previously said: "I can't stop it.. I can't stop it..I can't stop it."

Starting to wring her hands over and over in her lap, she declared she was a nurse. When asked what she was doing with her hands she replied, " I'm washing them... washing the germs off.. everyone's got the plague.. I won't get it if I wash my hands".

She described the smells and sounds of the patients and how unpleasant it was at that time, all the while wringing her hands over and over. She described having to try and feed the poor souls, to keep them clean and how this one and that one were almost dead and she was just watching it happen, day after day after day.

Moving on she described how she herself contracted the disease, she put her hand to her face to feel the sores she was describing there, she knew what this meant, she was soon to die to, she knew how quickly it would happen and the sorts of things she would feel and experience and there was nothing she could do about it. She felt powerless, surrounded by the dead and dying, herself now one of that number too.

Her last thoughts were of unbridled sadness and weakness; "Complete and utter hopelessness".

Once she was in the afterlife, she wanted to bathe her own wounds and to heal her damaged skin as she had described vividly the sores and symptoms she had suffered. As a woman proud of her position and appearance this had bothered her deeply right up to the point where she was too ill to care anymore.

Paula was aware of her spirit guides and wanted to call them in to gain a better insight around the meaning and purpose of that lifetime. They showed her "I had to realise I could not control everything, it was not up to me to try and heal everybody. My expectations were so high; no one could have met them. And to an extent I do that now. I am hardest on myself most of all".

Ruby's experience started with an unsettling feeling in the solar plexus area and her legs were feeling "sort of trembly". She was encouraged to go with the feelings and to move her position if she felt that would help in any way, she shifted, coiling up into the foetal position. "Yeh, I feel safer now.. but my hands are shaky".

When asked what her hands were doing she replied" protecting something...hiding my feelings..hiding my fear."

Prompted to go back to the first time she felt this, Ruby talked of her legs feeling "weak and pathetic...I'm useless!"

Ruby would resist going with the process every now and then but was encouraged to stay with it. She then recounted being "a female, weak, dependent and pathetic, I don't like it.... I can see Dad's face".

Her hands were now circling round and round over her stomach and she had now laid on to her back. As I watched it was as if energy was building around her centre, it felt angry and sore, hot and bothered, as I looked, I saw in my mind an angry little character stomping round and round in circles there.

It transpired that Ruby was angry, so angry in that life and previous similar existences. She was angry at life, at her parents at herself. And she was still angry, for in this current lifetime she had sought therapy for the terrible rages she would fly into. She was angry at being angry.

In the spirit realm she was able to call in her guides to help her make sense of things. To see the anger and all the people and situations where it seemed to explode and cause damage. It seemed there was somehow a genetic thread that bled down the family line and some ancestor work was required. She did not want her own children's lives to be blighted the way she felt hers had.

"I'm tired of being angry..so tired of it now."

Although this was not a magic wand type cure, she was pleased she had been able to finally openly talk about and share something that caused her a great deal of pain and shame. She saw there were choices she could make, to allow people to help her and to not try and keep it hidden, for it was never really hidden at all.

Seeing the possibility of her two daughters being affected in a similar way, gave her the resolve to seek her own treatment and therapy so that she herself could leave a more peaceful life.

There are no fixed agendas in the spirit world, no rights or wrongs, each of us instinctively knows what we need and what feels right. Who we want to see and what we need to give us strength, courage and healing. We can call in guides, loved ones, power animals, spirits and angels even. We can swim in healing waters, dive into crystal pools or dance to the beat of a magical drum. Here our spirits dance, free, bathing in the love and beauty of the universe. We can touch our spirits and let them touch us, for we are never not connected in this vibrant world of light.

19 INTEGRATION

At the end of the session, as the client comes back to the here and now, we will talk about similarities, the people, traits or personalities they recognise. They start the more conscious process of assimilating and processing what they have experienced. This of course goes on for some time afterwards as integration, like grief and mourning don't have fixed schedules.

What's important is that we allow time and opportunity to consolidate what we have seen and learnt. This allows our conscious mind to make sense of what the subconscious has shown it.

As a form of self discovery and appreciation, it is the key to understanding; being able to see any patterns or correlations, any similarities at all. It's this integration that makes the therapy so worthwhile and productive. Often clients are encouraged to keep a journal in the following few days as more insights can arise after the event.

Depending on the work done and the degree of trance and dissociation etc, some energy work or recommendations of simple physical exercise etc are also given; to ground the energy securely into the body. And there is always the offer to speak with the therapist with any questions, comments or concerns. So often things come to mind and questions pop up hours or days after the event and it's nice to be able to have that extra contact.

I hope you have enjoyed reading this book and the journey through some amazing past life stories. If it stirs something inside you, to experience your own past lives then I sincerely hope you enjoy them as much as I have. Possibly enjoy is not the right word but you know what I mean. Regression will not appeal to everyone and it may not be until some time in the future that it crosses your path again but hopefully this has provided an insight into what you might expect and what it might feel like.

Here's a lovely poem describing the energy of the spirit, the essence that rests in us all and which for me underlies the purpose of past life regression.

"Profound and tranquil, free from complexity,

Uncompounded luminous clarity,

Beyond the mind of conceptual ideas;

This is the depth of the mind of the Victorious Ones.

In this there is not a thing to be removed,

Nor anything that needs to be added.

It is merely the immaculate

Looking naturally at itself".

Nyoshul Khenpo Rinpoche

The Tibetan Book of Living and Dying

BIBLIOGRAPHY

Andy Tomlinson   *An Insight Into Past Life Regression*

Sogyal Rinpoche   *The Tibetan Book of Living and Dying*

Recommended Reading

Hands of Light - A Guide to Healing Through The Human Energy Field -Barbara Ann Brennan

Vibrational Medicine Richard Gerber, M.D

The Biology of Belief - Unleashing the Power of Consciousness, Matter & Miracles Bruce H.Lipton, PH.D

Journey of Souls Michael Newton, PH.D.

Other Titles by D DeSilver

Chakra Balancing - A Practical Guide to Balance the Chakras & Start Chakra healing Today

Chakra Awakening - A Beginners Guide to the Chakras

The Human Aura - Reading Auras & Colours

ON THE FOLLOWING PAGES THERE ARE A FEW PREVIEW CHAPTERS

PREVIEW CHAPTERS:

CHAKRA BALANCING -
A PRACTICAL GUIDE TO BALANCE THE
CHAKRAS & START CHAKRA HEALING
TODAY

Can You Talk The Language of Energy?

An Introduction to the Chakras:

Chakra is an ancient Sanskrit term, it's translated meaning is 'spinning disc' or 'wheel'. More often than not, when we are talking about the chakras of the human body, we tend to be referring to the main seven chakras of the human energy system. (There are more, but for simplicity we will focus on the main seven here).

Despite the ancient unveiling and naming of the chakras, it has been a relatively recent discovery that each of the major chakras resides very close to an important nerve plexus or centre, within the body.

It's important to keep in mind that the chakras are not things you can see or touch, they are not part of your physical body but they *are* part of your energetic body. To me, they are doorways, connecting your conscious and subconscious minds, as well as connecting your energetic and physical body.

The healers and seers of ancient times perceived that these seven major energy hubs or centres, were positioned along the human spine, from the very bottom vertebra, right to the topmost point of the head. They described the energy at these points as spinning. Similar to the motion you see where two volumes of water converge and a whirlpool is created.

The locations of the seven main Chakras are:

- The Base or Root Chakra - The base of the spine
- The Sacral or Second Chakra - The lower abdomen, about a hand width from your navel
- The Third Chakra or Solar Plexus - Resides around the navel and slightly above it
- The Fourth or Heart Chakra - Obviously this is located in the chest area
- The Fifth or Throat Chakra - This energy centre is situated at the throat, and affects the neck region as a whole
- The Sixth Chakra or Third Eye -Located between and slightly above the eyebrows
- The Seventh or Crown Chakra - This uppermost Chakra is positioned at the top of the head

They may not be tangible nor something you have spent a lot of time thinking about but you can certainly become more aware of the existence of the chakra energies. You can become more sensitive to how they feel and then go on to interpret the energetic signals they are constantly giving out.

Every one of the seven chakras vibrates at a unique frequency; its own particular resonance. One of the ways we distinguish them most easily is by colour.

- Red is the colour of the Root Chakra
- Orange for the Sacral Chakra
- Yellow for the Third Chakra/Solar Plexus
- Green for the Heart Chakra
- Blue for the Throat Chakra
- Indigo for the Sixth Chakra/Third Eye
- Violet for the Seventh/Crown Chakra

The energy of the human body is constantly communicating and therefore has a language. It is a language we can all converse in subconsciously. When you can *consciously* understand and communicate with it, then you are in a position to know yourself at a much deeper level, using and directing energy to sustain and improve your general health and wellbeing.

The energy flows from the main centres along minuscule channels, each nourishing and feeding particular areas of the body. Each centre is also associated with the endocrine glands, these regulate many of the main functioning systems of your body, working directly with the hormones. The types of functions affected are: your general energy levels, respiration, reproduction, overall growth and development.

You may have heard about the chakras being out of alignment or balance, maybe even closed. They are constantly regulating your energy, attempting a state of homeostasis, just as the physical body does. Your energetic 'body' is doing the same, it wants a balanced and stable sense of equilibrium. It will strive to maintain a sense of balance as best it can. Being in balance is the optimum healthy state.

The chakras can reveal themselves as being out of balance in a variety of ways. They may spin very slowly, almost unevenly, they may run very fast. The energy can feel weak or may be backing up, coming to a head. A bit like most things in life, we can get away with it for a while. Having an out of balance chakra may not appear to be too significant or important. But as in life, everything does have an effect and compensations will be made, energy may be taken from other sources, and other areas may start to be affected.

Our energy system is similar to our immune system, it can be strong or weak, and any point in between! It is constantly working for our optimum performance and protection. It is possible and in my opinion, more than likely, that a weaker chakra centre is where a physical symptom or problem is going to find it easiest to take hold. It may be in the form of an illness or disease or stress and tension or even an accident and injury.

Metaphysically speaking, areas of the body reveal psychosomatic symptoms and triggers, which can reveal the underlying implications of what is really going on. This is intricately connected with your subconscious thoughts, what your subconscious <u>believes</u> to be true and the subsequent messages it is giving your body. When our minds take hold of something as true, regardless of whether it actually **is** a truth or not, it sets a chain of actions in motion, to reinforce that thought and make it a concrete reality.

It's not just your mind that the chakras connect to. They are also in constant communication with your mental health and emotional wellbeing, not to mention the spiritual aspect of your being. They can reveal so much about us, on so many levels. Regular attention to the chakras and your energy system as a whole can help you achieve a much better level of overall health and a sense of holistic wellbeing.

One thing is a given. Your energy speaks the truth - it doesn't lie. It doesn't smooth over the cracks or say what it thinks you might want to hear - it is quietly broadcasting 24 hours a day in subtle ways - and what it communicates is always the truth.

This is one of the reasons I love energy work so much - it's a bit like working with animals, it is what it is and it does what it does. It is very pure and simple, if there is an imbalance or weakness, it will show it. The magic is in deciphering what it is revealing and that requires an honest and open mind.

In this book, we cover a general, broad overview of the main energy centres and indicators of what it would feel like to be in balance for each chakra. We also highlight some of the most common signs and symptoms of imbalance. Then you'll find there are a few suggestions of simple and practical ways to bring balance back to each one of your chakras.

It's Not Just About Balance

Tip the Energy Scales in Your Favour

Don't waste your time on a one - off balance. It's simply not enough.

Lots of people think they are helping themselves by getting into the chakras and think that the odd chakra balance or energy treatment is going to do the job. Just as one trip to the hairdresser won't keep your style looking good for long, neither will the odd half-hearted energy balance. But don't be put off either. There are a great many simple yet effective things you can do and probably to a degree already are doing that can really help your energy system.

The more you make things simple and easy, the more likely you are at being able to sustain it and reap the long term benefits. If you can also make your energy work enjoyable, then the more likely it is you'll find time to fit it into your busy schedule. So then it becomes a part of your regular routine.

The chakras are an integral part of your health. To remain physically healthy you need to eat and act healthily - it is exactly the same with your energetic health. For optimum effect incorporate chakra balancing, breath work or meditating as a part of your regular daily or weekly routine. It shouldn't be a chore as it can be an extremely enjoyable and relaxing, totally therapeutic process! You certainly don't want to be too compulsive or regimental about it either, energy work needs to flow and be fluid. It should be a natural and enjoyable part of your week, that's why I like to include practical and simple methods as they are far more likely to get done.

Not many of us live our lives in balance all the time, floating on a lovely fluffy cloud just above 'real world land'. No, we live in the modern world, with all the wonderful things it brings as well as all the not so wonderful. We have demands on our time, our energy, our pockets and our patience. Keep things as real and practical and as easy to do as you can. To start with, try swapping 30 minutes of TV time for a meditation or relaxation class. The benefits to your body can be immediate.

In a deep state of relaxation, the mind can be so receptive and immensely powerful. It is a direct route to tap into our amazing potential of healing and creativity. Successful business people, sports men and women the world over, use the power of their mind to achieve all sorts of amazing things in their lives. A great many people have healed themselves of all manner of different illnesses and diseases. You don't need to wait until you're unwell to harness this power.

We all have the ability and the potential. For many of us though, it can seem counter intuitive to take time out from our busy lives and if we don't see an immediate effect we decide it's not working and go back to old habits and routines. We get comfortable in our discomfort. It doesn't have to be that way.

Harness the power of your core, your inner self and your chakra energy to find the clarity of thought, the peace of mind and the wisdom to live your life more fulfilled, happy and at ease than you ever imagined was possible. Just make it more likely to happen by establishing new, fun habits that feed and nourish you. Things that balance your energy and positively feed it, without you having to think too much about it.

Learn to speak the language of energy and understand what it is trying to tell you.

Chakra Energy - Where Does it Come From?

There is energy all around us, in everything we can see and in everything we can't. There's energy in the trees, in plants, in our lights and buildings. There's energy in nature herself, trees have a different energy to mountains, the sea has a different energy to earth. Many people are familiar with crystals and can appreciate that they each have their own unique energy too. Everything has its own special frequency, even every individual plant and flower. It is this energy that makes homeopathy and aromatherapy so successful. So already you can see we are swimming in a universal soup of energy, we can't not be affected by it. This is how we are all connected. Not joined at the hip but swimming in the same big pond.

It doesn't stop there; each and every organ in the body and every illness have a different energy too. It's not just your physical movements and actions that have a frequency and an energetic effect, your words and thoughts do too.

Everything has its own unique frequency and energy vibration

This might seem a little hard to take but consider how you feel when you hear a beautiful hymn or a Christmas carol being sung. It lifts your spirit and makes you feel good inside. Now how does it feel when you hear harsh words, it usually sparks a completely different reaction inside. It doesn't feel good at all and it might even spark a fearful reaction in you. There is energy in those words, in their feeling and emotion. Emotions are our most powerful energy transmitters. We are reacting on an energetic level all the time. The chakras are our energy hubs; they constantly take in this energy and release it out.

As you might expect, some things are good for your energy and some things are not so great. Some things feed you and some detract from you. You will already have a pretty good idea of what does and doesn't work for you, even if you haven't outwardly acknowledged it before. You may even have noticed that some places feel comfortable and ok with you and some seem to make you feel on edge or your skin crawl. What is attractive and appealing to one, will not necessarily be the same for the next person. It is precisely because the energies are continually fluctuating, in and out that we need to understand them better. If we can work in harmony for more of the time and less against the flow, the better off we all will be.

If you can imagine the exchange of energy is as vital and as integral as breathing - in and out, in and out, 24- 7, then you can appreciate that a one - off energy balance won't do much good. Find ways that you know work for you, try some of the things I mention in this book, some you'll like and be drawn to and some you won't. What matters is, you find what works for you, and the things you know feed your energy, without having to drastically alter your life or abstain from the modern world and all the wonders it has to offer.

PREVIEW CHAPTERS:

THE HUMAN AURA- READING AURAS & COLOURS

Reading Auras

To read an aura, we need to appreciate what it is made of, it's past and its potential. We live in a vibratory universe, we were taught that at school, what we see and touch, although it may seem and feel fixed and solid, is made up of billions of tinier atoms and molecules, none of which are static.

Don't worry you don't need to be scientific; this book is anything but scientific. But the human spirit, you as a person, an entity, you don't finish at your skin. One thing that makes us so very human is our emotions, good, bad and indifferent. These feelings and emotions all have an energy to them, you know you have felt things about people, without them having to say a word. You can feel the different energy in a word said in a venomous way and the beautiful energy in a wonderful hymn or uplifting song.

Really it's not about learning how to read, it's about learning how the information is put together. You learn the process and as you get your thinking mind out of the way by keeping it busy with concentrating on what it knows, you open yourself up so you can more clearly interpret what's really going on, using more of your subconscious mind.

But in order to be able to do that we need to have some basic framework to build from and I am hoping I can really start from the basics in this initial book and if it interests you, it can be something you will build on and you'll evolve in your own personal way with it.

To successfully read and understand the aura, you almost need to be able to wear each colour as a cloak and with that cloak comes its own particular characteristics and personality traits. Now that's not to say each Red person is exactly the same, just as with any personality traits, that is not so, there is a potential of similarities and areas of interest that may be the same.

What is important is that you know the potential areas, the aspects that usually sit hand in hand with each colour and the corresponding chakra. With this bank of knowledge, your mind will have far more to pull from, when you are ready to read the aura. Then what you will find is that you are instinctively drawn to the aspects that are relevant and important for each individual client.

Just as if you were reading similarities between men and women and areas of interest for example, broadly speaking we might say that men are more interested in football and motor sports than women. That doesn't mean that no women are interested in either of those things. When you are working with the aura and any psychic related area, it is important to set aside your own assumptions and judgements, this is about honestly and cleanly accepting information that is there, without adding your own personal slant to it.

That is where things can go wrong, where misguided good intentions can be misleading and you might find people cannot relate to what it is you have to say.

It can be hard, certainly initially to be brave enough to just say what comes into your mind, but give it a go and just trust as much as you can. I know when I started I held back so often, only to find that had I been brave enough to verbalise the images and impressions I was getting, the client could perfectly relate to what I'd seen.

On the converse don't get drawn into the trap of just making anything up and letting your imagination run riot. You'll soon know what is relevant, certain areas will stand out more than others and as you look deeper, short stories unfold that the person in front of you can relate to. In that story will be some learning, some understanding for that person, regardless of whether they want to share that with you or not, so don't look for answers and fixed results. It doesn't need to make sense for you - just them. Be content with a nod of the head, be careful not to probe into situations or events that are none of your concern, unless the client wishes to delve deeper themselves.

You also need to be very sensitive and aware of what you are saying, more so when you are reading at a deeper level, as some very emotional and fragile things can come up, which the client may or may not wish to discuss. Remember this is not a therapy, there is no 'fixing' involved and I would set your intention to keep things light hearted, certainly whilst learning this skill. Although reading auras for me is more than entertainment, for our purposes here, we'll keep it at the fun and entertaining level!

Don't block your progress by expecting to have to see a brightly coloured bubble around every person. That's just your own need for proof, let it go. Try not to have fixed expectations, just be open to taking in this knowledge, using it as a guide and then start sharing what you see with your family and friends. Have fun with it!

The Human Energy System

The Human Energy Body

In energy terms, we speak of different bodies, subtle energy systems; not only do we have the physical body but we have the emotional, the mental and the spiritual body as well.

These fit together very much like the systems within our physical frame, we have the muscular system, the skeletal system, the endocrine system and the respiratory system. They all fit together and merge, to sustain the whole body, well so it is with the energy body.

It is always trying to maintain balance just like the human body; it is a perfect operating system. The energy body is fed by energy centres called chakras, these feed the aura, which is what you'll be reading and interpreting.

We can read it because whenever there's a malfunction or blockage or something is not right, the energy starts telling a story. When we look at that story it can be very revealing and insightful, to me it is just another way that your subconscious mind uses to bring things to your conscious attention and awareness.

We all got so clever and intelligent in our modern world, we thought we'd lost a lot of our intuitive senses, but we haven't lost them - we just haven't listened to them much. If you start listening and paying attention, you'll be amazed at what you can learn.

The human energy system is an amazing and intricate work of art. For our purposes here though, we will keep it simple. There are seven main centres in the energy body and it is these that feed and make up the aura. These go right from the base of the spine to the top of the head. These energy centres or chakras all work together, forever opening and closing, taking energy in, and giving it back-out. They are constantly sensing, they also resonate with specific sounds, and colours.

It is often one of these main seven colours that you will come across when reading auras, which are easy to remember as they are the colours of the rainbow:

Red, Orange, Yellow, Green, Blue, Indigo, Violet

I've also included brown, pink and white as these can confuse people.

You'll find there is a chapter on each of these colours, describing the personality traits and characteristics you might expect associated with them. These are not cast in stone but as you'll see, they will be your starting point and with each person, some of the attributes will feel relevant and will come to mind, and some won't.

We'll go through each of the colours, their attributes and traits, then we'll delve deeper into the body matrix, so that you have a good base of knowledge to call upon.

We'll also discuss a few ethical considerations and how you can sit in your energetic body in a place of compassion and non judgment so that you can far easily read and interpret someone else's energy and even you own.

Printed in Poland
by Amazon Fulfillment
Poland Sp. z o.o., Wrocław